LOVE'S DESIGN

Reaching Heaven on Earth

LOVE'S DESIGN

Reaching Heaven on Earth

SCOTT HIEGEL
Christopher Wrigley

PRECOCITY PRESS

Creative Director: Susan Shankin
Book Design and Layout: Barbara Gariby
Precocity Press, Los Angeles, CA

ISBN: 979-8-9873501-1-9
Library of Congress Control Number: 2022922137
First edition printed in the United States of America

DEDICATIONS

SCOTT

*To my mom, dad, daughter, and family, who showed me
what love is, as well as new family members Christopher,
Leslie, and Sue, who helped create this book, and to all
people endeavoring to bring love, compassion, kindness, and
understanding into the world at this critical time.*

CHRISTOPHER

*To my mom and dad, who brought me
from the stars to this beautiful planet.
To Sue, who picked up my hand and allowed
me to join the worlds of spirit and matter.*

FOREWORD

Sarah G. Schwartz

WHY MIGHT YOU BE INTERESTED IN READING THIS TEXT? Because our souls matter and because poetry is the language of our soul. This little gem of a book is filled with words and images that speak to the beauty and blessing, wonder and brilliance that we call Divine. Imagine our surprise in discovering that these gems are not far away, but are seeping through the very cracks and crevasses of our being, like sweet water from a mountain spring. How do we begin to search for this living water within and access it?

Through their unique life journeys, two individuals met and found unity in the discovery of this land of plenty, honey in the rock, heaven on Earth. In the poetic verses that came through them, they exchanged writings of what they each had gathered and witnessed in this inner Garden of Delight.

For Scott Hiegel, the door opened through a Kundalini experience that he believes is available to everyone and is the future evolution awaiting us all. I have not had the privilege of meeting Christopher Wrigley, his recently deceased mother Leslie Knighton, nor his special helper, Sue Near. Both of them have helped Christopher, with his immense physical challenges, to be able to share the gifts that are flowing from the depths of his heart. In this collaboration of beauty and humility, Scott and Christopher have poured out their offering for you in this grace-filled elegant exchange on the subject of Divine Love and Wisdom. Can the call of beauty and love truly save the world?

Every one of us matters, for we are all connected in our depths, and the Living Word that breathes through every one of us is LOVE .... Open the door, taste and see the wonder that awaits you!

Sarah G. Schwartz works as music educator, cellist, and certified therapeutic harpist. She has a keen interest in the work of Dr. Carl Jung, depth psychology, and the soul.

FOREWORD

Sue Near

HOLD THE HAND OF THOSE WHO CANNOT SPEAK. LISTEN. They will take you to a place of unimaginable beauty and great love.

My student has become my teacher and treasured friend.

I am deeply honored to have contributed, in a small way, to this volume of truly inspired writing.

Scott, you have now amplified the voice of the silent ones. All who read this book will be enriched.

I Give My Heart To You,

Sue Near, Supported Communication Practitioner

INTRODUCTION

IN THE SUMMER OF 2015, I SPOKE AT A SPIRITUALITY AND consciousness conference in Markdale, Ontario, Canada. My hope-filled talk described how certain life experiences, as well as recent profound changes in consciousness, had convinced me that we all have the Light of a stupendous Intelligence within us, and that we are hard-wired biologically to eventually reach a new heaven-like state of mind and existence. I call this the new Eden, or Heaven on Earth.

I ended my talk by reading several poetic verses that included breathtaking descriptions of our souls as the universe, and of the majestic and glorious states of higher awareness that await humanity through the further evolution of the human brain. The verses also spoke of the Love behind the universe and the eternal nature of our souls.

After I finished speaking, a young man by the name of Christopher Wrigley, assisted by a friend, came up to speak to me. I was startled initially because he was shaking and gyrating from side to side. I soon realized that Christopher had little speech. His friend, Sue Near, explained that my verses were meaningful to him, and that Christopher wrote about similar experiences. I was excited because I knew he understood the verses on a deep level and that he was a kindred spirit. This meeting turned out to be the beginning of a new friendship.

Cosmic Consciousness:
The Next Step of Humankind's Evolution

The conference I was speaking at was organized and hosted by the Institute for Consciousness Research (ICR-www.icrcanada.org). For more than 30 years the ICR has hosted an annual conference, and its members have worked tirelessly to raise awareness about the profound work of Indian sage, Gopi Krishna, and his revolutionary concept of Kundalini.

From his own experience, Gopi Krishna (1903–1984) posited that human evolution is planned and that individuals and the whole human race are evolving to a more beautiful, peaceful, and glorious state of awareness through the actions of a biological process and Intelligent Force in the human body and brain called "Kundalini." It is a state of awareness that Dr. Richard Maurice Bucke termed "Cosmic Consciousness" in his 1901 landmark book, *Cosmic Consciousness: A Study in the Evolution of the Human Mind*. Mr. Krishna further postulated that the Kundalini mechanism is also responsible in human beings for greater creativity and talent, genius, mystical experience, psychic phenomena, and in its unhealthy form, certain classes of mental illness.

I related to this theory through my own experiences and felt this was a Truth that would have an earth-shattering positive impact on the thinking and behavior of humankind.

In cosmic consciousness, one's awareness expands beyond the limitations of its five senses and intellect. A whole new view of creation opens up, and a whole new source of knowledge becomes directly accessible. The world now appears much more expansive, beautiful, and embracing. Eternal life swims into view.

The cosmic conscious mind has been referred to throughout history in the spiritual, religious, and secular literature of the world by various names including, Paradise, Bliss, Samadhi, Nirvana, the Holy Grail, the Fountain of Youth, and the Treasure Within. In Kundalini theory, these all represent a description of the same experience and represent the next step in humankind's evolution.

What amazingly hopeful news to realize that the potential of Kundalini and the cosmic conscious mind reside in each of us.

I believe learning to love and serve others is critical to achieving this new state of awareness, and that new worlds of beauty, light, and intelligence will open up to humanity's sight once we learn to make love our primary goal in life. Finally, experiencing an all-encompassing Love and Unity is the goal of this next state of evolution and we need each other's help to reach this next level of reality.

The Genesis of this Book

A number of years later at another ICR conference, I was able to renew my friendship with Christopher's devoted mother Leslie Knighton, and his very special helper, Sue Near. By this time, I knew Christopher wrote profoundly moving poetry and had an uplifting story to tell. I also realized I wanted to help give voice to his inspiring life. Although limited in speech, and slowly losing his vision and body coordination, Christopher's mind burns brightly. With his penetrating inner vision, he sees ethereal realms of beauty and light, and his being overflows with love and wisdom.

Sue is able to crystallize Christopher's otherworldly inner visions and profound insights into beautifully flowing streams of inspirational and poetically moving words. Sue described her process of working with Christopher as follows: "Christopher and I have always worked hand over hand to type his thoughts on the computer. When we first began, we listened to music by The Proclaimers, and typed with rhythm. As we type with full attention and trust, we establish a brain connection and are able to share thoughts. Christopher learned to touch-type which has allowed him to continue to type as his vision has diminished."

Sue shared some of Christopher's writings with me over the years. Eventually, this sharing metamorphosed into the idea of exchanging our love poetry in a small book, adorning our poetic words with touching pictures of love and majestic scenery, as well as awe-inspiring images from the universe.

We all believe that Christopher represents a powerful spokesperson for people with disabilities, as well as an inspiration to all people. We feel our love poetry is an example of the immense wisdom and creative potential that lie untapped within the minds and souls of us all. It also demonstrates how such jewels of inspiration can be more easily and powerfully created when we work together in service and cooperation.

I think most of us would agree that the world at this time needs new answers to its many pressing problems, as well as a greater influx of hope and love.

GOPI KRISHNA said, "The love you give, the service you do, the help you render is the food of the soul. It is immortal."

GANDHI said, "Love is the strongest force the world possesses and yet it is the humblest imaginable."

MARTIN LUTHER KING JR. said, "Darkness cannot drive out darkness. Only Light can do that. Hate cannot drive out hate, only love can do that."

WALTER RUSSELL said, "If you put love into everything you say or do, love will come back to you in the measure of your giving."

CHRISTOPHER, SUE, LESLIE, AND I know that our learning to love and serve more deeply and universally is one important answer to the problems of humankind.

We all believe there is a Loving Intelligence behind this creation and Love is our ultimate destination. We are put here in this world to learn to love and serve. We need to develop the capacity to love to its fullest extent. We have not even begun to grasp how powerful this force can become in helping to effect positive change in society, as well as to heal ourselves and the world.

Everyone has a unique love story to share. I hope these love exchanges inspire people to share their own love poetry with others, as well as their experiences of love. Sharing love transcends all differences of race, religion, country, gender, economic class, social status, and physical form. Sharing our love can help us better see our common humanity and divinity, help us see past our human dualities and divisions, help us see ourselves as part of an undivided whole, and finally help us see more clearly the love in each of us. Along with sharing love, comes peace, wisdom, freedom, and truth.

These poetic verses also share glimpses into this marvelous new state of understanding, awareness, love, joy, and peace that awaits each one of us someday—the cosmic conscious mind.

I was raised in Madison, Wisconsin and come from a family of six sisters and one brother. When I was a young boy, I dreamed of becoming a professional golfer or basketball player. Somewhat disappointingly, these dreams didn't materialize, and instead, I became an accountant, an investment professional, and entrepreneur. I eventually discovered these professions were not the end of the road for me, but rather were stepping stones to new dreams and my life purpose. If somebody had told me thirty years ago when I was feverishly trying to climb the ladder in the financial industry, that this once shy Catholic boy would write a book with a disabled man from Canada, sharing love poetry, as well as inspiring experiences of higher states of awareness, I would have laughed and thought they were crazy!

Christopher wrote, "I am honored to have you as a reader of my work and my attempt at the expression of greater understandings received by myself and others living in bodies which have limited functioning in this earthly existence. Love has kept me cradled in its arm these long years. It has nurtured me and been my teacher. It has nourished me and made me strong. It has sung to me and eased my pain. It has brought people like Sue, my mother, and many others of great promise into my life and now it has brought you."

Christopher and I have found that life will always have surprises. If you want to give the universe a good laugh, just tell it your life plan! We believe you can ask for guidance on how to fulfill your passion and dreams. I know this is one area where the universe has satisfied the dreams of both Christopher and me in writing this book. We sincerely hope that you enjoy it, and that it inspires you to share your love with others and to live a more joyous, peaceful and love-filled life.

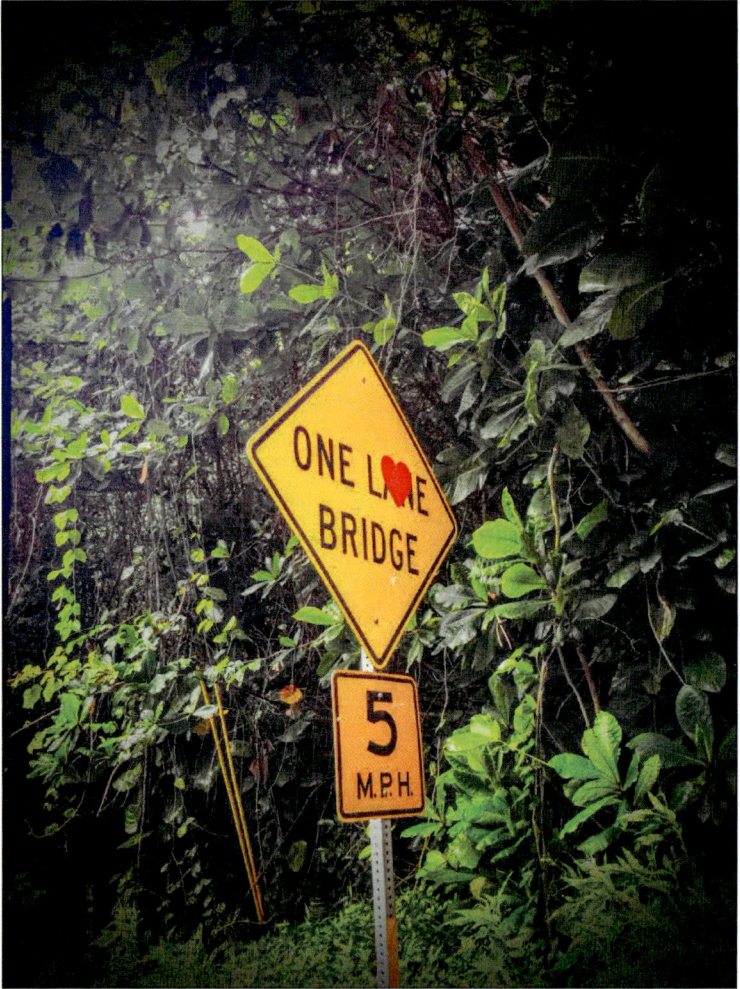

1. CHRISTOPHER'S LOVE SHARING

Dear Scott,

Love is the source of all that is good. It is the force behind heartfelt emotions benefitting earth-kind. It is a renewable resource plentiful and ever intensifying as it is called upon. It burns more brightly than any star and will be the prime factor in any solution to problems facing us now and in lives to come.

Love can be considered a measure of growth in society. Where you find Love and compassion, you will discover comparable peace, health, and well-being. Love is the generator of positive action. You may realize this in your daily work and in society, but remarkably, it is equally apparent in the lives of individuals. Love promotes healthy decisions and strengthens convictions. It allows us to find courage and develop confidence. Most of all, it eases pain and suffering. This message is sent to you with Love and in truth. Truth is Love's guardian.

I am feeling the warmth of Love's energy as I sit beside my friend of great passion right now. Love is, above all, about passion. Passion leads to compassion when it is directed toward others. When an individual singles out another person while in the state of Love, a union is formed. Love may wander, which is its nature. Like the universe itself, it is ever expanding. If the union remains strong through dedicated action, it becomes a creative and sustaining force. Dedication to an idea, an art, or a scientific pursuit guided by Love's passion results in tremendous accomplishments. The work you have taken in perpetuating the power of Love itself will bring unification with those you speak with every day. I have done my best to remain loving in my daily life. I have felt Love's passion. May we all practice loving, for when it truly becomes human nature, we will live our lives unbounded, and possibilities will never cease.

I give my heart to you.

1. SCOTT'S LOVE SHARING RESPONSE

Dear Christopher,

This creation is a play of love invented by an unimaginable Loving Intelligence. We are the actors in the play. Achieving a oneness with creation, realizing our eternal nature, and experiencing a permanent Love beyond our physical senses is the goal of this next state of evolution.

It's important that we build an environment that allows for the healthy development of Love and the unfolding of our cosmic conscious sense. The practice of sound physical, mental, and spiritual disciplines, the cultivation of eternal values like love, kindness, compassion, truth, and service to others, the creation of a clean and life-sustaining living

Grave of Alcoholics Anonymous (AA) Co-Founder — Dr. Bob

environment, as well as the adherence to time-honored moral and ethical principles, are all critical components to achieving this goal.

I think it is important that we help each other to love, create, and unify rather than hate, compete, and divide. It begins with us. I hope we can all become **Love activists**

ESA / Hubble

and do the work to change and purify ourselves and become who we are meant to be. When we create love, peace, and harmony within ourselves, this allows us to bring love, peace, and harmony to the world. As we purify ourselves and share love, this can have a ripple effect and lead to positive change in others and in the world.

The healing and love that takes center stage as our inner beings of love unfold, eventually transcends all the pain, loss, and destruction, that has taken place in physical reality.

Closer and closer to Love we move, for eternity. We reach new and brighter shades of light, new dazzling displays of creativity, new levels of grandeur. We are jewels of creation transformed.

Love has also come to tell us that we never die; we only change form, for eternity. The future is bright. It can be trusted. We are all vessels of light, heirs to our eternal birthright, infinite love, peace, and joy.

2. CHRISTOPHER'S LOVE SHARING

Dear Scott,

When you are looking at the stars this night, watch for the twinkling star to the North. It will be your devoted friend Christopher, just winking. When I feel sad or lonely, the stars bring me peace. I am not able to say what I am thinking. It is my disability. The stars are like a thousand thoughts waiting to be expressed. I have placed them there. Now that I am writing to you, one of these stars has burst into fireballs to become bodies like the most glorious planet in the Universe. The earth holds great promise, for it passes through the light of our great Sun. The Sun is the source of energy which life must have to fulfill that promise. I imagine this as I sit beside the shores of Georgian Bay. These are just a few of my stargazing contemplations. The next star to ignite will be as a result of your reading this letter. When it is understood by others that I am truly the author, there will be a shower that will light the heavens, for all handicapped people will be celebrating.

Wishing Upon A Star.

ESA / Hubble

2. SCOTT'S LOVE SHARING RESPONSE

Dear Christopher,

It is a flaming love, a true love, everlasting in nature. Sown in human love, heaven's destiny arrives, a flaming love lit up in eternity that will light a new heaven, create a new earth, birth a new man and woman.

We are like two stars bursting into flames, uniting as one, setting in motion a fireball that lights up the earthly skies, rolls through the universe, reaches heaven, and leaves the citizens of heaven panting, stunned, and dazed.

It is a love of earthly origin, yet cosmic proportions, that starts as a small spark, gathers momentum, becomes a roaring flame, that creates a cosmic firestorm, that lights up the universe, streams beyond the universe to heaven, streaks across boundless heavens, reaches close to Love, and finds the true Light that is never extinguished, that never goes out—our true and everlasting home, our final destiny.

I hope someday the whole world will follow your lead, Christopher, and we all wish upon a star together. We need each other's love and support!

3. CHRISTOPHER'S LOVE SHARING

Dear Scott,

When Love enters a conversation between two people, the air surrounding them turns a color imperceptible to those individuals. It is so beautiful that forces of great magnitude are brought to attention. As the color intensifies, so too do the great light forces for goodness. The individuals are strengthened as they become better in mind and body. These people then attract others. This is how the world shall be transformed. Keep love foremost in your mind, speaking of love often.

The way to share a meaningful truth is through hugs of greeting, departure, and in consolation. Love is a vibration that is easily set in motion and requires only sustainable human-powered energy.

3. SCOTT'S LOVE SHARING RESPONSE

Dear Christopher,

I look out upon you and realize you are me. When you hurt, I hurt. When you grieve, I grieve. When you are joyful, I am joyful. When you love, I love. Soon no distinction is made. We are the same essence of an eternal Love that lights up the world, for eternity.

The following are two heavenly expressions of this deep and infinite Love existing within all of us:

To my mother—I have stepped through a portal in time and space to come upon an enchanting world where love and peace reign supreme. I hug you mom. Our souls weep, our hearts melt. We are back together, this time forever. Our love is no longer limited by time and space. We dance a waltz, sing a new tune, eternity is ensconced in our hearts—the sweet melody of love, peace, beauty, joy, and harmony. This is our true estate, our future inheritance. I am so moved, beyond tears, beyond pain.

To my dear friend—I squeeze your hand and look into your eyes; I see eternity. My heart jumps, my soul dances. I hold you tightly. I peer deep into your eyes. Your beautiful soul melts my heart. I have crossed the chasm, to a world of beauty beyond comprehension. I feel a love that I never want to let go of. My heart bursts, tears of joy flood my soul, time melts away, space disappears. I have touched love! I have touched Heaven here on Earth!

I skip, I float, I dance. I clutch both of your hands, my soul swoons, we are forever young. I release all the pain in my heart. Love returns, true love, everlasting love, tears of joy, waves of bliss. I will never let go. Our hearts are intertwined for all of eternity.

Christopher, we all need to follow your lead and share love freely. This will truly birth this deeper love, change the world and set us all free!

4. CHRISTOPHER'S LOVE SHARING

Dear Scott,

I am called Red. Blue is my last name. My best friend's name is Green Violet. We make an odd pair. Wherever we travel, we leave a rainbow. Have you followed us through the sky? We are most often seen following a storm but

if you look closely, you'll catch us where you find water cascading over a rocky cliff. In our existence we are but waves. It is a brief life in your terms but fleeting as it is, it is awe-inspiring to our kind. We live to bring beauty to this planet. Our cousins are vibrations that are sensed through the ears of earth's beings. Have you marched with them as you've paraded through town in celebration? Of course you've felt them as tears streamed from your eyes while you followed a bride's wedding passage. They are creators of deepest emotions. Without them you would find life has little meaning. All experience is associated with emotion. Together sound and color have made many pleasant memories. This is our legacy. As waves and vibrations subside, we are transformed, escaping gravitational forces to join others throughout the universe. When joining with other unimaginably magnificent vibrations and imperceptible colors, a swirling powerful stream emanates, and love is born. Love is the source of creation.

4. SCOTT'S LOVE SHARING RESPONSE

Dear Christopher,

We have come home to a place that is beyond time
And space, a place of eternal beauty and rest,
A place where the human and divine merge in a
Timelessness that creates a space of merciful Love.

A Love that never forgets; never holds on,
An all-encompassing Love that holds all of our
Failings lightly; We have come home to a place
Beyond space and time, where our identities merge
With the eternal substance called Love.

Now I no longer exist; personalities disappear and
We merge into the cosmic space that holds all in Love.
This is our true inheritance; our deepest calling is to merge
With Love to become one with creation.

Now we know our true self that exists in you and you in me.
We are no longer separate, separated by vales of tears,
But we are the perfume of cosmic holiness
That reaches out in Love, embraces all in Love,
And creates a space for all to unite.

Eric Whitacre's Virtual Choir 3: Water Night

The Virtual Choir is a global phenomenon that brings together singers and their love of music. Singers record and upload their videos from locations all over the world. Each one of the videos is then synchronized and combined into one single performance.

5. CHRISTOPHER'S LOVE SHARING

Dear Scott,

The way people are going to experience greater love in their lives is if we as a species try to open our minds to more ideas granted to us from different energy sources. I will explain. We are now limited in thinking by living a busy life full of chatter, most of which is repetitive and unrelenting. When we are in quiet contemplation, especially in surroundings of the natural world, we make ourselves available to these energies. Observe hikers in the forests or children on a beach building dream castles in the sand. Feelings of wonder and joy abound.

Another source of magnificent uplifting contemplation is through listening to music, or better still, to be singing or playing an instrument.

As these feelings are created, they must either be expressed outward or stored in the mind and heart. Those with deeply fundamental stores of love, and those overflowing with peaceful energies, are ones who will create the highly valued currency in our universe. This, of course, is Love.

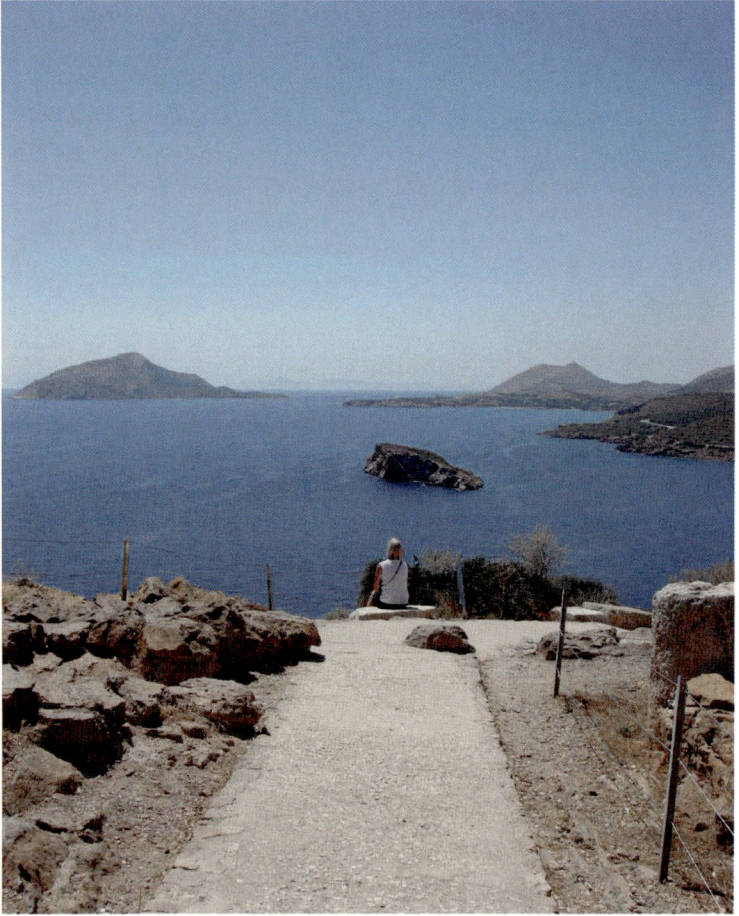

5. SCOTT'S LOVE SHARING RESPONSE

Dear Christopher,

I'm sitting on a bench overlooking the Wapsipinicon River, just outside Davenport, Iowa. It's a cool summer day. A gentle breeze is blowing. I have completely let go of time. Time is eternal in the moment. I let go of all expectations. There is no need to rush. I'm thinking of you, Christopher, and Love.

I realize Love is waiting in the moment.
When I flee the moment, I flee Love.
When I stay, the moment turns into eternity.

When I flee the moment, I vote for fear, rather than trust, thinking safety comes from the world, rather than from Love.

When I leave the moment, I leave the present — the presence of Love. I leave the eternal for the future or past. I no longer am present because I have left the present. I am like a ghost fleeing. I am gone, fleeing to the next moment, which never arrives.

Now I return home, to my true home. I am forever at peace in the eternal presence of Love.

Christopher, it is important to realize the great truth of the Light within that is guiding us. Let the music flow in life and don't fight—flow! There is a harmony of which our inner voice mirrors and leads.

We can make great music in this life, whether it is being a janitor cleaning the floor, a violinist, a teacher, or hospital worker. We all make music in different ways. When we are in harmony, our bodies will speak. They will glow in the inner truth that is being expressed.

The key to life is to listen and make music to our own inner heart. It is to encourage all people to let them know of the possibilities that they have within.

We are meant to be sons and daughters of Love. We can never give up on ourselves or put limits on the potential that we have. Listen to the inner ray of Light that says that diversity is great, that accepting ourselves and all people, including our differences, is in harmony with truth.

Never give up on people. There is the seed of Love in each of us. It may be covered up by sorrow, trouble, despair, or conflict, but it is there. Spread the message of this truth through the actions of our lives. There could be no better example of inner truth.

Finally Christopher, as our lives demonstrate, the further we go inside of our minds, the deeper into the mystery we penetrate. We enter a new world, a new existence. Reality becomes so soothing, so peaceful, nothing looks the same — a silvery radiance, a sparkling sea of consciousness. Our true inheritance is a gleaming, glittering, majestic, sea of throbbing, living, vibrant consciousness.

Form disappears into eternity. We float in this sea of consciousness, graced beyond words, a sweet melody encased in Love. The deep longings of our heart are filled in this sea of Love.

Hidden in creation are new layers of creation, beyond the probe of our senses. Hidden in form is formlessness. All of a sudden, the door opens and a new layer of creation is revealed, embedded in an existing layer; so simple, yet so profound, the key to the mystery. One can only enter on Love's terms. One does not enter by force, or by self-will — a complete yielding to Love is necessary. We must be cleansed of all impurities, all selfish tendencies.

Beyond the probe of our senses, the veil is lifted. Now we see a new layer of creation is revealed, a new layer of existence; so simple, so incredible, so profound; all done with Love's infinite grace. Love has opened the door to its greatest prize — eternal life.

ESA / Hubble

6. CHRISTOPHER'S LOVE SHARING

Dear Scott,

I have been thinking about you, my friend, and about our previous discourses focusing on the essence of love. I have been dreaming about the time when all earthly beings justify their actions based upon their love for society. In this period, each individual will be raised by families who give great amounts of energy to their local communities. Equally important will be their dedication to every creature in their environment.

Children will hear messages of love and affection, feel the warmth from the touch of all arms that hold them, and see faces radiating joy and great happiness. These children will be carried home to places designed to provide all the essentials to nurture this earliest awakening of love.

Music will be the first food in a diet consisting of things of beauty. Play and work will be important as children begin to gain the simple skills needed to contribute to life. Schools will teach tolerance, cooperation, and peaceful resolution in matters of disagreement.

We have reached the time of change. We have come upon the moment of love's expression in all lives. It has arrived and through efforts by people such as you, it will be manifested in our time, in our lives.

I give my heart to you.

6. SCOTT'S LOVE SHARING RESPONSE

Dear Christopher,

I long for the day when we can all do this for each other! The "Children" you previously mentioned is the whole human race. We can start right now, one person at a time, led by your words of Love.

Soon we will come home. Then we will see Love face to face. We will cry out in joy, knowing that we have found our true place in the universe.

We will know that Love was always close, always protecting us. We will know that our hearts were always filled with Love. We just had to pick away the mud to reveal the glittering diamond that has always shone brightly.

Love has always spoken the truth. We are now getting the ears to hear this truth, which is located in the deepest center of our heart. There resides our soul, our lifeline to Love. We have never been separated from this. It has always been brimming with Love.

Soon we will see Love. We will see that the creation was created for love and harmony. Our star will shine brightly. It will speak of Love through its essence. Separation will end and the creation will be brought to its fruition. Love will have spoken. Time will cease but Love will remain.

We will have come home. All the living parts of the creation will have become one. We will not cease. We will be melded into Love, one continuous living organism pulsating with Love. We will not die but will be transformed and melded into the Living Light. Each of our stars will shine brightly. We will be like jewels shining for eternity.

From chaos to Love, the creation will have fulfilled its destiny to bring us all back into Love.

ESA / Hubble

MOTHER EARTH
What Matters Most

When I asked myself *What is the matter? What matters most?* a poem arose in 2017, which I will share portions of here because it just might matter. . . .

You are the matter of our being. This womb of life I'm clearly seeing is a jewel of love beyond compare, welcoming all if we but dare to hear your call to save our Earth, for future beings you will one day birth . . . .

Diversity is your middle name, so much wonder, never the same where the Spirit breathes life through every cell, calling us all to wake and be well!

What can I do to help bring peace so the gifts of life might find release? The opposites are dualities. Let's rise above them if you please . . . .

How do we open our eyes to see, that love is about harmony?

Can Alchemy's secret transformation bring us to a new creation?

Heaven on Earth is humanity's dream, let the stars descend in a light-filled stream! Earth is a treasure of rarest being, and living here is full of meaning . . . .

I wait in the space for the healing third, as I listen to the sweet song of the birds. What's the new thought that may arise, to lead us to the dawn of sunrise?

I love you, Mother, ring the bell that tolls for you in the sacred swell.

—*Sarah G. Schwartz*

ACKNOWLEDGEMENTS

TO SARAH G. SCHWARTZ

What a gift to meet and know you. Your friendship, love, and support have meant so much. You have helped me to share my deepest truths through my writings. Your sharp eye for editing, keen intuitive sense of what to include, humble goodness, just plain kindness, thoughtfulness, and constant encouragement helped to make this little book a reality for Christopher and me.

TO MY BROTHER MARK

Since we were little boys, you've always been there helping, protecting, and supporting me. From the days of playing as kids, to climbing the ladders of business success and material achievement, through the dark valleys of life's struggles and challenges, and now to the pursuit of love, happiness, and our true life purposes, you've been right beside me. You helped shape the content of this book of Hope and Love with all your wisdom, insights, and common sense.

AND FINALLY TO LOVE

I never knew that you—the unseen, the eternal, and truly real—could be such a dear friend, tough taskmaster, gentle inspirer, true guide, and sweet and tender lover. I now know that a part of me will always be a part of you, will always endure, and you truly are my home sweet home! This book is inspired by you, the true everlasting love and foundation behind this universe.

ABOUT THE AUTHORS

SCOTT HIEGEL lives in La Quinta, CA, and runs a consulting and investment banking business called Solquest. He has a BBA from the University of Wisconsin and an MBA from UCLA. He's been a former CPA, CFA, Vice President of Corporate Finance, and entrepreneur.

He enjoys writing and talking about his experiences with Kundalini, and his lifelong roller coaster and, at times, perilous search for inner peace, the Divine, Love, and higher consciousness. Through speaking, outreach, film, poetry, and other creative expression, his goal is to entertain and inform people about the gifts and profound importance of Gopi Krishna's work, Kundalini, higher states of consciousness, and Love.

His interests include visiting museums and historical sites, traveling, listening to holiday music and oldies, and watching movies. He enjoys sports, hiking, and attending 12-step meetings. He loves reading books about spirituality and the inspirational people who have helped make the world a better place.

CHRISTOPHER WRIGLEY was born in Markdale, Ontario on July 3, 1975. Shortly thereafter, he was taken to Toronto, Ontario, for heart surgery. Over the years Christopher has been cared for by loving parents, Leslie Knighton (deceased) and Paul Wrigley, and adored grandmother, Marge Shorthouse (deceased). He currently resides in a congregate home maintained and supported by Community Living Meaford in Ontario.

Christopher attended public schools near his home through a program developed by the Special Education Department. He was included and welcomed in many mainstream classes, but often found himself in segregated classes as well, due to his physical and communication challenges.

He is a creative and skilled communicator, using gestures and facial expressions, signing, thumbs up and down, laughter, and his limited speech. It was in the mid-nineties that Christopher was first provided hand support to access the computer. It opened a whole new world for both Christopher and staff alike. He is an observer of the world and listens attentively to those around him, following the news, his many sports teams, and the arts—particularly music—on TV and CBC RADIO.

Christopher is now able to share his deepest understanding and to advocate for those without a voice.

Finally in his own words, Christopher wanted to share the following:

"The way to real happiness is to be the friend of someone who is locked away. You will be releasing them from darkness, bringing their spirit into the Light. Once freed, the spirit will expand, touching all people in need and even those in plenty. You, of course, will be carried by love and gain new strength for further work.

My greatest lesson comes from my inclusion in community.

Let the days of your life be filled with good wishes, for all good wishes are those most influential, and travel at universal speed.

I give my heart to each member of the worldwide family.

Christopher Wrigley—born to hug."

To learn more about Scott's personal story, Kundalini experiences, transformed consciousness, and poetic verses, please read his book *Reaching Heaven on Earth: A Soul's Journey Home,* which is available on Amazon or at Booklocker.com.

For further information regarding Gopi Krishna and Kundalini theory, please visit the Institute for Consciousness Research (ICR) at www.icrcanada.org. Scott also highly recommends reading *Living with Kundalini: The Autobiography of Gopi Krishna,* as well as Michael Bradford's book *Consciousness: The New Paradigm.* Michael's book may be found on Amazon.

For further information on Supported Communication, please email Sue Near at suenear13@hotmail.com.

Finally, to share your love with Christopher or Scott, please email us at shiegel@verizon.net.

LIST OF PHOTO CREDITS

Manufactured by Amazon.ca
Bolton, ON